The Psychic Girl

Calico Dawn

An intuitives journey from impact

and isolation to celebrating gifts,

holding space and finding joy

Published by Chiral Clarity Ltd

Cover Image Photo by Seth Doyle on Unsplash

ISBN: 978-0-473-49351-6

Dedicated to all the intuitives who have travelled this journey and all who will follow.

Our collective consciousness has access to such great love. It is a privilege and a blessing to support each other along the way.

Contents

Chapter 1

Internalisation and Isolation

I knew a girl who was born with all of her gifts open and clear, so that for many years they threatened to overwhelm and break her. She did not feel rare or special instead the impact of them left her feeling confused, nervous, terrified, alone, ugly and unwanted. But what she would do with this experience would bring healing and support to others on an intuitives journey.

This was a sweet young girl, growing up on a farm with a diverse and ever-changing family. Her perfect day involved an early morning start with the house to herself and all the views out of the windows were of quiet dawn over hills and trees for as far as she could see. These moments were always precious as it is in the still of the dawn hour that the energy of the earth and sky seem to meet, sharing stories and bringing in a calm knowledge that most people do not take the time to hear, while she could almost feel it in her body.

For a girl like her it was also the only time in the house that she did not feel exposed to other people`s energies, emotions and manipulations. She had learnt as young as her memories could reach that being aware of what other people were thinking and feeling was the best way to feel like there was some semblance of control she held over her own body and safety. While this was a necessary self defence mechanism many sensitive people learn naturally to cultivate hers had no boundaries and so she was always fully aware of others as they went through the gambit of all of their realities each day.

It would be very many years before she became conscious of the fact that people didn't actually say all of the things she thought they did, only thought these things, and learning to trust in humanity again was about believing that it is not what is thought that makes a person but what they choose to do and say with those myriad of thoughts and ideas. When people are hurting they think anything that may give them a feeling of empowerment, and when people are in distress these thoughts can be deep and dark. It is a very necessary piece to our psyche that we can find alternatives to our realities, adapt and fight for life. These thoughts themselves are not bad but if they appear to be reality to another then they become very heavy indeed.

So, she would bask in the morning stillness, taking the time to gather herself inside for strength and to reach her energy out to the land for support and a link to love. This land was her home and her heart was in each of the paths, hills, springs and trees, most especially in the animals. She spent many hours outside of school just wandering on her own or with siblings, playing with grass and sticks, simply being with her imagination in this space.

Other times she would be with her horse, leaning up against it while she talked to herself or the horse, using her tiny feet as grips to scramble up its forelegs and just ambling around on its back until called into the house or the mare startled and caused the girl to topple off, as she regularly did. It was very rare that anyone would attend to the animal or take time to add saddle or bridle so most of their hours together were spent idling away time in this way until a real ride was possible.

School days were always fine as this girl never minded work or travelling, being home or out. Whichever was the space she found herself was the place she was that day. When she arrived home, she would race the others to the chores, feeding animals and cleaning and collecting pocket money with a practical focus that pleased the other kids too as they preferred not to do these tasks whenever possible.

But spending time with the chickens, talking to them each morning and night, was a very nice way for her to spend her time when these were also her friends. Each animal had its place in her heart and though it was hard to see the larger ones go, as happens in farm life, she was devoted to these animals which bought her joy.

One morning in winter, when she was calling her friends out of their cage to their breakfast, she noticed one was missing. He was the loudest and cockiest of them all so to not be at home was startling to her. She walked the house grounds until she came across him and sat beside him and cried. The adults were unconcerned and did not offer time or energy towards the girl`s reaction, as he was considered unimportant and little more than a hassle in their mind.

So, she sat with him until the school bus arrived, and came to terms with him leaving. When she returned after school he was gone, and the feeding of the chickens became one of the chores she left for the others after that.

In the spring the local school encouraged children to train and present various farm animals. Dairy farmers would have calves for their children to hand rear and sheep farms would have lambs. She was unaware that these lambs were orphans, and this was really just a mutual service the farm owners provided local children in return for the hours of hand feeding they were going to do. The girl thought that hers was her pet. She spent many hours each day feeding and brushing and trying to convince the tiny lamb to learn tricks from a very small girl who did not know how to train it. When the school day came to bring your animals and she saw that so many were well trained, but her family`s ones were not. She felt ashamed that she had not known what to do.

When spring was over and the lambs were fully grown and ate grass now, she came home one day to find her lamb gone, the farmer having collected it, and she did not get to say goodbye.

The next spring she was given a new lamb. She used the same name as before, hoping to create a bond and re-enact the time she had given her last baby lamb. Whether the girl`s expectation for connection was uncomfortable for the animal, or she carried the events of the year in her aura this time, the animal was even less obedient, and she sometimes would yell at it and say the mean things that repeated in her own day back at this animal. In the annual show the lamb was even worse and did not do even the simple things they had practiced. She was sadder now and felt certain it was because she was no good at this.

Her falls from her horse had increased too over the year, and although the mare always stayed right beside her and nuzzled an apology, she started to cry to the horse and ask it why it was mean to her and did it hate her or just want to pick on her as everyone else did? Why didn`t her mare love her anymore? But as it stayed so close and seemed very caring to the girl after her falls the girl wondered maybe her mare didn't mean it and it was her mistake not the horse`s that had caused it. She would have to do better at being on guard around her friend now, hold on and be very aware that she was now a nervous horse.

One day she had scrambled up onto its broad back, holding onto her mane and very alert, determined to watch for anything that would make the horse shy. She was fearful of every twitch or snort now and the horse of course began to feel uncomfortable with the girl as her tension, fears and anxieties grew over the years. As all beings are entitled to, the horse began to deal with its discomfort by avoiding the energy by removing the problem. Over time it became harder for the girl to get to the horse, she moved away a lot and the girl worried she was hurting the horse`s leg climbing up it, so would marshal another child for boosts up instead whenever she could. One time she tried to get the horse to the fence to climb up, but the horse leaned into the fence to brush her off and the sharp top of the fence cut into her legs, so she did not do this again. The horse began to move under low hanging branches to remove the nervous child from its back or shy or run haphazardly then leap to the side, leaving the girl in mid-air for a moment before tumbling over its rear or off the side to the ground.

Over time the girl mostly sat in the grass near her horse talking to it or pleading with someone she couldn`t see to prove their existence, so she knew she was not unwanted or alone.

A third year there was another spring lamb and she carried its name on once more. She tried to only love this animal and hope it may decide to do some tricks if she was kind enough with it. She fed it by hand for many mornings and nights and loved that it trusted her and came each time. She would play with this friend and walk around the yard with it and it happily led the girl around as it ate grass and listened to her talk to the horse and the man in the sky who never answered her back.

On the school farm day the girl and her lamb did well even though she was not able to enjoy that, as by then she understood her friend was to go soon, and it had taken her three years to do what the other children seemed to manage easily, unaware that they had parents who guided them or people showing them what to do.

She did not believe there was any person who she knew was there for her. Her grandmother Rose was not far away. She never came to the house and her mother did not talk to Rose either, but she was always there right when things might have gone too far and would quietly move her arm around the girl and distract her so that she didn't absorb the true memories of many things over her early years. Rose was very quiet and never seemed to say much or even talk with the girl. She just came by when the girl was low and tried to show her she was loved and supported. But the girl did not go visit her grandmother as this had never been done, so it was only those moments where Rose came by that her granddaughter was aware of her.

But every time that she was sad or low Rose was nearby or offering what support she could from afar.

Over the last few years her family had changed many times. In her early memories there was a dog and a father that did not come with them to the farm. Then other people came and went from the house too. Sometimes they would stay briefly a few days or a night. Also, the girl and her siblings would go and stay with aunts, so they were not left alone in the house.

For some time, another family lived there too, and their energy was very strange to the girl. One time they sat with her as they all camped and told ghost stories. She had never been afraid of things at night, but the eldest son was telling her about evil things and people who are angry and come back for revenge. At the same time, he finished his punch line something became visible in the same space. As if his talking about the possibilities had triggered an opening, she both saw and felt this new thing in the room. And though it had a human form, her terror from his story and the isolation of being away from home distressed her greatly and she rolled the two as one event for half of her life. From then on, the awareness of things in rooms with her grew and though her grandmother tried to calm her and hold her hand when she was scared it never stopped the fear returning like she felt that first time. Why would grown-ups tell her there was nothing there and then expect her to trust them? Who was she supposed to believe when no one saw what you saw so they decided she was imagining these things? How do you feel safe if there is nothing you can do to stop this but hide under blankets and wait until morning before you can sleep?

This other family sent off strange thoughts and feelings that the girl saw as stories. They seemed both angry and sad at the same time. Sometimes the boys would be kind and she felt sorry for them that their father was unkind. Other times they were brutal or scary and their mother would yell and make small things into big things that the girl was told she should have known.

It was much better when they felt stronger and moved on to a big house of their own, but the girl had learnt that there were so many things she did not know that were important rules. This left her feeling that she could never know which thing she was expected to know the next time, and a fear she would be yelled at for being stupid or ugly or uncivilised. Many times after that, as she ate a meal, she would worry about the spoon in the sugar bowl, or fear having to eat foods over and over that made her whole body shake or using all the hot water.

Some of the winters had trips away to stay with a series of relatives. She was with one lady who tried to be nice. But the girl did not see her this way, as all of her anger and resentment showed in the way she held her face, or her body or maybe the girl just read her thoughts again. The aunt was not cruel just very bitter and unwell. She tried to make the girl feel safe by adding pudding to the meal, which was a very rare event in this child's life. But when the girl put the spoon up to her lips her body flinched, and she did not want to eat this. The aunt corrected her fear that it was bad and, while disappointed in the reaction, tried to persuade her to try the chocolate dessert that was her own favourite, and she ate some happily. The girl tried and her whole body began to shake, and her vision blurred. She didn't want to eat it and accused her aunt of poisoning her. It did not go well for anyone that night and in long sight became a very good lesson to the girl about everyone having an agenda but no one being wrong; in it turned out that her diabetic aunt could only have artificial sweeteners, whereas the girl was terribly reactive to these chemicals.

Each winter that the girl`s mother was away she stayed with other cousins, each time going to a new school. Having to be included even though it was temporary was something she picked up from the teachers` and principal`s thoughts each time. She tried hard, learnt the songs or participated in lessons but mostly spent these weeks on her own unless a sibling came to this house too which was rare.

One winter she stayed with older cousins who had children of their own. There were people to play with and many people slept in this house. There was a terrible storm and the girl who had only known low laying farmland was very scared to be in a house, built on poles on the hill, which was facing the open sea in cyclone season. As the house moved beneath her, she became so consumed with fear and thoughts of the end of the world in this great storm that she did not sleep well that night or many nights after that. She was now always unsure when a storm would come that was strong enough to move the house, and she catastrophized that if Dorothy` house got swept up could hers too? The people in this house did not think anything of these regular storms in their environment and did not know how much time the girl spent with these thoughts in her head. She did not sleep much that winter as most nights were wet and windy, and over the next few days she became impolite, combative and difficult.

Though she enjoyed being in this house with young people and food she had never seen before that was plain and not vegetables, she was never invited back to that house and always missed the nice mother who loved her children and always tried to smile even though she worried a lot and had very kindly asked her to try to be good and mind her manners. In one of the many alternative experiences of this lifetime she was coached by this lady in using cutlery to eat no matter what and when taken to a meal on this holiday she was presented with drumsticks and doggedly used only cutlery, to the chagrin of the lovely mother, as the girl was not prepared to make a mistake after being schooled so carefully for the visit.

In between winters the girl`s own family had made the decision to leave her farm and move into town. The girl yelled and cried pleaded desperately to be able to stay. She loved this land and it was home in her heart. She could stay by herself here or get a tent even. What was the point of life if you were not where you are meant to be? But the move into town was inevitable and the promised trips back to visit did not come to pass. A long time later she went back to the farm with someone else and she saw her horse in the paddock, but when she called her the mare looked up but did not come to the girl. She was not wanted there.

In this town surrounded by other houses you were not supposed to walk into, and where you could hear fathers who yelled as much as the girl`s mother did, she felt her heart break. She began to walk also, as though her legs still remembered the freedom of walking cross the farm all day. She would walk to the next town and back or down her road, past the shop to a park where she found a very old oak tree for solace. She could spend many hours up in this tree. It had big broad branches and her petite feet could grip the knolls to climb up the way she had with her horse when they were together. Her body enjoyed the memory of this and the walking and climbing, but the girl mostly wrote songs up in that tree and only occasionally asked the man in the sky for anything now.

When it rained she could walk around for hours as the raindrops masked her tears, and no one ever seemed to notice this young person wandering through the rain or hiding up a tree. There did not seem to be much point to life when you knew you would be sad forever. Or worse alone and sad.

Chapter 2

Independence and Friendships

An important thing for the girl was when her grandfather Leo moved in with the family. He also missed the farm and was a very patient man. He quietly went about his life watching out for the girl and finding things he needed that she could do. He would find chores for her so she could have some pocket money; he would let her cook his dinner even though she did not know how to cook and make his lunches each day so she would feel important. When she got bossy or mean or did not do a very good job, he simply ate the food and few days later would ask if he could have only a little bit on his sandwiches or perhaps poke the cooking food to see if it is soft before it got too soft. She did not eat the food she cooked him as these were vegetables she did not know, and while Leo would try and share little bits, she could not cope with fearing not liking them so could not bring herself to try.

Mostly the girl ate rice and porridge which she had learned to cook and sometimes she would try and make some baking like they had done in a school class. It never worked out the way other baking seemed to, but she did not know why. She only tried these foods when she was really hungry or wanted to have something sweet. She never felt good when she ate sandwiches and she did not know what else to do. Mostly she did not eat lunch or would buy a sweet bubbly drink if she had money. It seemed to fill her up for a short while, so she started to do that most days if she could.

The school had a system of everyone taking turns in the shop where people could order bought lunches, and when she learned how to use the system for a small extra donut, she stayed fuller for longer. Then the man who ran the school let her know that he would do a double check before and after each day too, so she stopped doing that before she got into trouble and just bought the drink when she could.

She was lucky that she was able to move schools one year. Her sisters were not doing well and it was causing problems for them. Her older sister was very unhappy too and no one seemed to like her; people were mean to her at school and she was always sadder when her little sisters asked her for help she could not offer. Her other sister got upset very easily and the teachers made her sad and mad and silly. Sometimes teachers would just yell at her little sister and other times, when she was injured or upset, they would not listen and made her feel she was a bother. So, the girl made sure that they moved to a new school so her sisters could have a better chance of being looked after. It was a wonderful thing as all the sisters decided that they would become new people. They would pretend to be a new person to these new people and maybe they would like them.

Her older sister always changed her name after that with each set of people she knew. She had learned that when she did not feel good enough, she would just pretend she was someone else. At her funeral people spoke of her with so many different names, they all understood that she helped many people in her short life but also the she never found herself.

The other sister did not do well with pretence and found it easier to rely on the girl to simply get her in and out of situations rather than trying. She was not more confident for being in a new environment, but at least they were new and interesting. The school was so small everyone had to get along and the girls finally made some friends.

The girl was never sure if her acting was so good that these people did not know the real her. She was strong and loud and confident to them all and her new friends were all loud and smiley people too.

One time the girls had a joint birthday party, and each

had one friend come. The girl's friend also bought a gift for the other sister which was very kind. But the girl was not happy that her friend's attention had halved and felt very strange inside. What if her friends liked the sister more than her and one day didn't like her anymore? She made sure her friends were very different to the people her sister liked so she did not have to worry that they would like her better or want to include her in anything too. Although she understood her friends' thoughts that she was trying to do the polite thing, the girl was uneasy around actions for politeness and became more direct and reactive than ever.

Now she was a teenager she was also up until late into the night talking to friends on the phone or reading books and began to get less patient again.

Her moods got worse every year. She was always tired in the mornings and soon she began to get terrible headaches. She craved sweet drinks when her head hurt but it only made it worse and she had more days with headaches than without. This would be her reality for many years, and she learned to enjoy her friends when she was well and tried to avoid talking and being around them when she was not. Her friends were often cautious of her moods now. Her kindness was still there, and her understanding of what people felt and thought. She could see the stories behind them of what had happened, so many friends found comfort talking to her on those good days. She was very honest and attentive when her friends were in need but felt great anger to their parents who put their children in these positions. Her anger at them, at teachers who did not want to teach and at bosses who just wanted to boss, often gained very direct retorts from her or nasty looks. This did not leave the girl feeling welcome or valued at all, as they responded to her dark moods with unease or reactions of their own that the girl received loud and clear.

As she was very smart and used her awareness to learn but also to navigate teachers no one called any attention to her strange behaviours. Even into high school her extreme derision to teachers and people who befriended her sister would perplex people, but her grades meant she was not of enough concern to get involved. It was only near the end of her school years that anyone asked her to stop this behaviour. She considered their request to be heartfelt so listened and decided to try. Teacher and sisters were much happier, but the girl felt like she had failed at everything, so she did not feel better for this. Now she didn't even have the feeling that came when you made someone do or feel something really big, only a paleness of who she was.

Alongside these changes in body, school and peers her grandfather always talked quietly and patiently with her. Sometimes she would challenge this with outrageous things or break the law to show him he should not trust her. Other times she would ignore him or tell him he had no place to tell her anything and it was all none of his business. And though he was sad he would leave her be but never leave her alone. He took great comfort when she was bossy with him or made him drink water or worried if he had eaten. He did not mind her trying to feel in charge and did not make her feel bad as she got older and went away for days to her friends.

When she was nearly finished with school Leo went to stay with some other family. One day he rang, so she got to him to tell him how mad she was that he had not come home yet. He came to visit the very next day and he looked very tired and thin. The girl got very angry and yelled a lot that these people were not looking after him. She made him sit while she made him a sandwich and got him water to drink and demanded he come home. He smiled and ate his sandwich and hugged her goodbye as he warmly always had. He seemed to believe he had to go back to them and told her he was happy there and they were nice to him, but she could tell how unhappy was by his face and body and that he wanted to come back to her. But she was young too and didn`t want to have to be looking after him so agreed he should go back after all.

Her mother called her a few weeks later from one of her trips to say that Leo had passed away, but that she didn`t think the girl should go to the funeral as it would be hard so not to worry about that. She had decided it was easier to not look after Leo so had not given the girl knowledge of his grave illness, and the girl only knew she had decided not to bother making him come home. She also worried she had not told him for so long that she loved him that maybe her grandfather had not known that she really did. She wished so many times after that that she had had time to talk and make sure he knew how important he was to her. At any rate he was gone now, and she did not have anyone at home who noticed what she did anymore, so she would get on with her life on her own, as that was how it was going to be anyway.

Chapter 3

Drama and Disassociation

She had many people to spend time with if she wanted. She listened to all their problems and saw all their histories like stories and could offer ideas or clarity or came up with connections from uncovered secrets that seemed obvious to her. She stood behind her friends no matter what they thought or did or said because she knew them inside and out and they were allowed to be who they are. Sometimes at a party she would play a game by telling someone at the beginning of the night everything that would happen that night or week. This person would get with that person and it would last only so long...Or they would fight tonight and break up, or someone was going to trip on the stairs tonight. People started to be uncomfortable around her so she would sit to the side and watch it all unfold. There was an emptiness at seeing things after you already knew of them that felt almost disconnected.

To her there seemed to be little point to life when it was always so predictable and obvious what each step would be. She did not consider looking at her own path to see if it would improve, but perhaps it`s better she did not know all that was coming as she grew up. Feeling sad and uninspired made her question if the was any point to even being here to witness it all unfold.

She began to play with this information and sabotage lines of stories she saw, or trick people into doing things to see if she could. She even tried to trick herself by making decisions that did not do anything for her or undermined options just so she could be rebellious and on her own terms. Relationships chosen this way did not work well, of course.

She even began to fear relationships as she saw more and more of her life unfold in stories. The girl understood if she got married and settled down that this would go very badly and all the things in her next few decades that would be a struggle became things to resist too. She would simply never get married, have children, go to University or buy a house. This would solve the anxiety that built around the stories she could see. Better to stay alone than risk what looked to be coming.

Tricking herself in and out of things became more confusing and she tried to dull these thoughts. She found the drinking made it quiet in her head for the night and sometimes it was easier to just have a break from it. A bit like a holiday, sometimes these breaks needed to come early in the afternoon. Once she tried first thing in the morning to drink and dull the thoughts in her head. She was fortunate that a man who loved her was brave enough to say that he did not think this was ever OK, as she could easily be cruel when she was criticised. She did hear him and agreed, though often felt like she had gotten that situation wrong and embarrassed herself. She did not come away feeling cool, she felt foolish and separate that people saw that happen. Even now to hear "It`s always 5 o`clock somewhere" takes her back to those feelings and she feels a failure and that her faux pas was a very big deal.

Getting it wrong still made her feel in danger of violence or worse: people thinking horrible things and throwing those thoughts and feelings at her. Even if she is the only one in the room, getting it wrong makes her feel she should have known better. The feeling that came off the lady who lived with them on the farm, and who had screamed terrible things at her when she got things wrong, still overwhelmed her heart each time she is unprepared in a situation or did not realise something someone else already understood. It is such a shock to not know something when she usually knew everything that this left her feeling exposed and unsuccessful. Always less than she was, and she did not feel she was much to start with. Most of her life was spent with this dialog of sadness, loss and despair and the people around her were also in such despair that there was no other version to see herself in, no way of giving this feeling back to those who felt it. To only do her own feelings would have been lighter but she did not know that these were not about her or that anyone held any value in her being here.

For some years there were also substances that could lift you or make you do and say things that were different to what you did before.   At the beginning it felt good for the girl to be detached and not have to think or feel everything. But each time it was many days before she felt better than low and many days in thinking dark and lonely thoughts. She realised that it was worse to stop the information briefly and be overpowered by it afterwards and stopped playing with most substances to regain some emotional balance.

Over time her body became more tired and malnourished and illness manifested in her body, trying to show her the need for hydration and food and nutrition in order to survive. But it would take some time before she felt she was worth fighting for.

Illness, fatigue and sadness were constant companions. Isolation from family then friends and struggling with the terrible headaches that followed any deep and moving conversations. She loved these interactions that went on for hours, and the deep, penetrating energy and focus she had begun to rely on feeling, to make her empowered and to use this intensity to feel alive and perhaps have some value too. But the recovery from this extreme engagement also took their toll on her body and mind, unable to sustain these brooding connections and still interact with the energies of everyday life. So, she went home each day after work and slept. She slept on the bus, on her desk at work and any moment she was not moving her body would shut down.

Chapter 4

A Body`s Communication

There was a blessing when she met other people with great fatigue. It was watching other people like this give up and have no life that made the girl realise she might want to participate in this life after all.

Doctors did not support her in this journey. They felt her ability to work negated the illness underestimating her early work ethic on the farm that had instilled the getting up and going to work. She tried many versions of body workers and stimulants.

One day she met a lady doing natural medicine. This woman was a doctor in her home country, but explained she had turned her back on western medicine because she believed she had better version now. The energy rang so clearly from this person that the girl felt her whole body vibrate with a feeling of hope and goodness. The woman simply pressed a metal bar to the girl`s hand while she held things and did not hurt her or make her feel stupid. She talked about her life and learning and how no one knows this stuff, and the girl felt safe instead of ignorant and just a little bit curious.

It was so interesting that she diligently tested every single thing in her kitchen and all but the rice depleted her energy. Many years on and she still had not learned to feed herself. So, for a few years she ate mostly rice again. If she went out with other people, she only ordered hot chips and nothing more, she felt foolish and poor and noticed their sympathy with embarrassment but was determined that only the things that were good for her were going to be in her future.

In those days there were not many alternative foods or much knowledge of allergies and she simply kept on with basic food and added in vegetables she was familiar with, salads too and meat and rice. Very quickly the fatigue lifted, and she realised the impact it had on her. Everything she ate or touched affected her body immediately, from food to chemicals to temperature. She became aware of needing to notice what happened to her body with all of these things. The naturopath woman had unwittingly become a mentor, giving the girl the idea she was worth looking after and was allowed to do things for her body that was good.

After a few years of not eating intolerant foods her body was strong and vibrant. She had learned to drink water and the headaches went away. Each time she became unwell she observed the foods and learned to witness these effects then later to use her energy sensitivity to test the energetic effect on her body before eating this.

Even though her relationships were not going well, and she was very alert for criticism, still she was at least listening to her body, learning she has a voice and a choice and to choose her best self. When she did not choose wisely, she also got the opportunity to observe the consequences and sometimes work backwards to find new ways to put down what was not good for her body.

Another healer who crossed her path brought her face to face with her emotional state and released her from many programmes that she had been reacting to. With gentle strength, kindness and a resolute system of breath release she held space for the girl to find these truths and release them. What other people thought or emoted towards her still hurt and made her nervous, but she no longer reacted with such hurt and anger to things, feeling she was not going to survive other people's anger or strong emotions. People around her became calmer as she did, and she found many of the people she had journeyed with really did hold her kindness and time to great value and they shared love and time with her too as she healed.

Chapter 5

Mediumship Forms

A year or so after one sister had passed suddenly, she was woken from a very deep sleep thinking someone had come into the room. Her hyperawareness of energy and fear of the dark had not lessoned over time, just her emotional reactiveness. In the dark and alone was always a scary time for her. Some relationship decisions were based solely on the need to not be alone in the dark.

She called for her partner and he was not in the room, but he come when she yelled loudly for him. Even with him in the room the energy did not dissipate. It felt like waves of anger and hatred rolling at her. Terrified and confused she could not get her partner to understand, and though he tried to make her realise there was nothing in the room she knew there was.

This occurrence led her to a medium who was able to identify this as her lost sister and she took the time to explain things about passing over as she understood it, sensitivities people have, suicide rates in intuitives, and shared a little of her own struggles with the girl.

Although they only caught up yearly for medium sessions this was the next time she found a mentor. Not that she was being actively mentored, but there was finally someone like her, who really knew what she was experiencing, had her own reactions and had struggled with it to have any kind of life. This gave her hope that she could find a way to live with this and not in fear. To know there were others not only like her but also who suffered so deeply made the girl feel that perhaps it was not that there was something wrong with her, but that perhaps this was the same for very many people.

Time and relationships moved forward and she found herself in a position she had hoped to avoid by not committing to a permanent relationship. When she was young a friend had asked her if she wanted to get married and the girl had responded without thinking how she thought that would go. That she would be stuck in a relationship she could not leave, because they had a house & kids together, with a man who was unkind. She could almost feel the emotional turmoil of being in a manipulative and unsafe place again with someone she thought she should have been able to trust. She had avoided this for many years.

But realisation began to dawn on her about the partner

she was now with, and the unhealthy thoughts, paranoia and controls that were appearing one by one. Like the peeling of pages in a picture book, each one revealed more irrational temperament and behaviours. She began to think she may be crazy. He told her she was and acted so sure in his assertions. There were no considerations or allowances and when called on these things the energy became dark and unbalanced like a lightning storm, waiting to see where and how the shock would manifest. His justified certainty that he should be able to do as he pleased, and offence and rage when the girl argued with these made her wonder if he was right. His energy was so overpowering in his righteousness that she felt the obligation to believe him in her body every time, at odds with her head which was so confusing. His energy felt sure and maybe if he believed it so strongly then she really was wrong.

She knew that things were not good and tried to ask for help. She found a counsellor and began to tell her the situation. She requested coping tools and told the lady she needed someone to talk to, as she could not financially leave the house. The counsellor listened and gave her some distancing tools, but did not agree with the way the girl was coping by compartmentalising. She did not believe the girl would stay if it were true or that anyone would be functioning intellectually if it were real. It was several sessions in before she heard the girl and finally understood the story. She told the girl to contact a support network immediately and so the girl did. It was unfortunate that they could not help her until she gave up the house and so she was back to waiting.

Once more she began drinking. Each day when she came home from work to make the evenings go faster and to help her to not react or to not take in what he was saying and feeling. After a while it became two drinks; one to get through to dinner and one to take care of after dinner. This went on for many months and she managed to keep going with her life as it continued around her.

Many nights she would be unable to sleep and would sit on the deck looking over the lawn to where the light finished reaching, or up to the stars and question how she had ended up here after avoiding this very thing her whole life. She would write letters she could not send to the sister who had passed and cry and worry and shake with the stress she carried.

On one night she was outside late at night thinking about another drink to help her sleep when she realised what she was doing. She almost felt as though someone was sitting with her asking her questions. It was in the family to become addicted to drinking, did she really want to activate that gene?

Was the best solution to someone not taking care of her to harm her own body? If you attract things in your life at your own level was this what she secretly thought she was worth? Each thought or question felt like a strange feeling inside her head, like she was remembering something that had never been said and a feeling she could not grasp like the atmosphere around her body thickened just a little. It was like a memory and a tiny feeling of certainty at the same time

She had not thought this way before, previously negotiating in her head the work or friends or family she had as a sign of positive self-esteem. But if this was what she really thought of herself the girl realised she had not looked that deeply. It was as if ego and worth were very different things and she had worked with bluff and bravado on her esteem but had never looked at her belief around her real worth.

The girl decided that this was not what she deserved. She rarely drank again after that unless she chose to in celebration. She looked at this idea of value and began to turn it around and around in her head. How was it possible to not know that you did not value yourself even though you told yourself you did? What kind of belief system did we have that would hide this truth from our consciousness?

They became long and deep thoughts and she focused

on making believe that she did think she deserved more than this. Maybe if she could talk herself into more worth her heart would catch up. It seemed backwards but also made sense to the girl, that if she had not realised how worthless she felt deep inside until that moment, then the solution was to work backwards towards that. The girl seemed to almost feel like she was sharing these thoughts with someone else, that the idea she was worth caring about was shared by others and even in tiny flutters and feelings she was beginning to feel the support of these others.

She continued to write the unsent letters to her sister and talked and puzzled late at night through her pen. It was like a conversation as she almost automatically wrote the answers or supportive things back to her tearful sentences. More and more the dialogue flowed, and she began to relax and enjoy this feeling of talking and sharing without any need for sound. The girl started to recognise a feeling of certainty that went with the writing, that she knew what was true and supportive. With her friends she would sit and talk to them in the same way sometimes, simply saying things that came to mind and not filtering or considering them unusual. Trusting the feeling of communication coming in and the loving energy it brought in with it, like sitting with a grandparent or old friend, and then sharing this information with her friends felt very uplifting.

Chapter 6

Clairvoyant Extension

It was only when her ex-partner accused her of making up stories about her friends lives and her friends believing them when she spoke that she became aware that these were not normal conversations. She had always seen and said things to people that were not openly shared or known, yet this seemed to be more of what was going on or coming up than simply what was going through someone`s mind.

While this was a piece of their relationship exit conversation, with support people in the room and giving up the house after all, she did not give it too much thought until later. It was the realisation that it was some kind of actual thing she did and not merely the conclusions she had always assumed were obvious, and this idea came and went in her mind over the next year or two

When she was re-settled, and distanced from the distress of that relationship, she went to see a clairvoyant. It was a woman she trusted and although they held different religious belief systems, she found that when this lady read her cards she did not speak from her personal view point. It was fascinating and accurate and delivered with great kindness. With many more decades of life experience she was able to temper some information and expand on others with some tact, but the older lady was always kind and so many things she had seen had come to pass.

This lady told the girl she should get some cards too and use them to help other people. The girl had always been uncomfortable with cards and runes and many things she had read about when she was a teenager. Her energy at that age had made it an easy tool to use to manage other people or to look at information that may not have been shared voluntarily. She felt so different from that earlier self that it seemed it may pull her back to old feelings if she used divination tools.

The lady understood she had fears here so did not press then, but a year later at the next reading she brought it up again. This time the girl had established a home and rented out rooms to young people beginning life. She had a safe environment here where she had complete say over a peaceful home away from others. It was very quiet and felt isolated and only people whose energy was welcome here even came to the house. It was an intention the girl had set when she first arrived, that she did not want to continue to be fearful or on guard about who could come to her home. She walked around her home and just thought over and over the thoughts that only those she would want here would be welcome, almost imagining others would feel uncomfortable and leave before they knocked on the door if they even made it up the long driveway. She pictured the image of the very energy of the land making people turn back. Not understanding how this worked just simply deciding what she would like to happen, it was an effective boundary system over many years.

Only people that suited the space and her energy came. Flatmates were sparse and while she learned that was to make sure she did not have many bad experiences it was limiting when sometimes no one even answered a room to let ad and money remained equally sparse. This became a good lesson of working with energy. She realised she needed to focus on what she wants it to feel like when one manifests something one wants, rather than simply writing out a few rules or lines, as so much gets missed when it is a decision made by the brain without the heart. She even started asking the energy around her to help her and to find ways to support her with this.

When the older lady brought up cards the next year she did so in terms of a choice of future income or continuing as she was. The girl was very uncertain about learning the cards and if she would be any good, the lady looked her in the eyes and said lightly that the girl could learn them if she liked but that neither of them really read the cards they just talked and let the cards guide them. A truth resonated in her body to these words and she believed the lady.

The girl thought about her reservations and insecurities but also about her deprived fridge and cupboards and realised she did not want this to continue on for more decades, with a fear of not having enough food and equally a fear of inexpensive foods that still impacted her body. The old lady had found a motivation that could override the girl`s fear. Though it would not be a successful business until the idea of money left her head, the girl began to study the cards, practice and found different ways to engage in them. Sometimes she would read a booklet, others she would interpret them from the textbooks she had read. Her friends would let her practice and once she started talking she forgot to check the books and started to talk and share and clarify situations for others.

When she was unsure, she would sit quietly for just a moment and almost look for something else to come around the corner. If it did not, she would pull another card and then it would clarify and become a bit clearer. Each time she did this it got easier and in time she would just breathe and reach then talk. Every time the feeling inside of certainty or joy would get stronger. After a couple of years it was clear and strong and felt natural to simply share this. The feedback had helped her insecurities but mostly it was that feeling of rightness the girl felt that motivated her now. To see the stress lift from someone when she spoke of what was really going on, or to confirm what they had already thought but had not been able to trust in themselves, was special. As though each time their self-worth got stronger and they too learned to trust themselves as they received confirmation what they were getting inklings of. She could almost see the agitated energies of her clients soothing, the stress in their vibrations softening and their ability to receive kindness a little more open too.

For some people it was just a few simple things they needed to hear, but for the girl the feeling of joy grew each time and it began to clarify as the love and support each client`s guides or ancestors brought into the room for their person. The feeling of absolute love and acceptance they shared that the girl was able to interpret, or fold the energy over people like a blanket, felt like a healing all on its own. This was a feeling the girl began to reach for too. Sometimes for her clients and sometimes for herself. To feel that she was supported and loved and worth loving began to be easier to believe in.

She began to look back over events in her life from this perspective of support, as if she could imagine that the feeling of kindness and love that came in when she connected could go back with her and hold space then too. The more she thought about events in her life this way the easier it was to see the value in each lesson.

Chapter 7

Healing and Holding Space

Over time this became a natural exercise to send back love when hard memories surfaced or even heavy thoughts of another person. Even if she knew she had been unkind, she started playing with the idea of sending kindness back to both her and the person. She could not ask forgiveness, but she could offer it to herself. If she had had the support then that she felt surrounded her now she would have been able to make better choices and not lash out at people. She understood this and was able to begin to release these old incidents as a measure of her worth.

An amazing thing happened when she did the same thing for memories of when other people had let her down. As she imagined them needing and receiving kindness in those moments she realised they would not have acted that way either. That their behaviour was not about how they saw her just about the pain they too had been going through. Like a great weight lifting she could almost drop the invisible cords that connected her to these people and the situations, disengaging them from her energy and releasing the access to her body.

The more she acknowledged, forgave, loved and released memories the more energy she had. It was as though these had imprinted on her and she had carried around this pain every day in her energy. Noticing that things can stay with, her she began to look at this in a more practical way.

She observed her family and client interactions. She noticed when she really felt badly for what a client or friend had gone through she almost followed the memory stream of their story and felt it through her body too as if she were experiencing this. She had always done this for clarity and understanding. Even when she was at school talking with her friends this feeling of having the experience in her body had occurred.

Now with the awareness of release she felt with disconnecting from old memories, she worried if she would be any good at supporting her clients if she did not use her body to experience their stories.

Her insecurity at not being able to reach for the information if she did not do it in her body took some time to overcome. First, she would practice releasing the information she had shared. It was not her information and she got better at disconnecting from it. At the end of each reading she found that she did not remember all of the conversation any more. Her mind was no longer full of all the information she had shared, and she was able to rest and recover faster after each one.

Then she recognised that the feelings in her body were not hers they belonged to the person she was working with. She practiced at disconnecting this too and dropping the energy off like unplugging a giant electric cable and throwing it over a cliff or out to sea. Once again she played with the idea of going back in time and disconnecting and tossing out the stories she had embodied to understand. She realised it was not her information and she did not need to store it in her mind or body.

With more practice and intentional thoughts she looked back at the other things that had made her feel heavy and sad. She once more looked at the idea of people treating her badly when they were hurting and noticed that this sensation of feeling like they threw their hurt and anger at her really did feel like an impact on her body. What if these impacts were to go too?

Over times of contemplation she played with these

ideas, noticing things that happened that were not about her at all, but were just people upset acting out their learned behaviours.

In the workplace this was the most obvious to her. These people were not her family, friends or clients so she did not feel an obligation to take care of them anymore. It was easier to stay one step removed from them, though now it was not to keep way from being impacted by their thoughts and moods, it was a choice to not take on board what was said or thought or felt by them. She noticed that if she did not take it personally, just disengaged from the energy, that the other people calmed down. It was like they only got worse if you reacted but if you did not react then they were able to recover themselves faster. Sometimes she would reach for a little more information and she would see that they had gotten insecure or scared and that was why they had reacted so badly. She started to offer the love and kindness energy into that space to support them, as she did clients, and found that not only did they calm down, but they seemed happier each time too.

As much as she was able to, she practiced not engaging with other people`s energy, allowing it to flow past her like clouds passing each other at different heights. Not only in not engaging with their energy but also not with their story. It was enough to hold space for them.

She did listen to their words and responded to these on a real-world basis. If there was something in these reactions that needed addressing she would of course take action. But first she waited to see if they did resonate with her; almost like her body could show her if it was right for her and would feel calm; or if it was not right for her then she would feel tired or uncomfortable. Just like many years before, when she started to notice the energy change in her body with different foods, she became aware this was the same with people too.

No one was bad, and it used a lot of energy to try and judge them or decide if they were good or bad, and was this really anyone`s right? But bad behaviour did not mean justified reactions. And no matter how righteous some acted, if it did not sit easily in her body then she did not take it onboard as her own truth anymore. Her energy and her body were her own and she could feel the peace and joy that came with trusting her instincts and choosing to listen to her heart instead of putting her needs last when someone had big feelings.

A lot of other things were coming out of this exercise of listening and checking things against herself. As she was working on these things in her head, she was also paying attention to the reactions in her body. Alongside every moment she checked in with herself she also felt more certainty about the information she was receiving. While she could not see them, she was more aware each day of her guides and ancestors around her.

Other spiritual people in her life had talked about them from her first medium to her clairvoyant lady. She found this idea fascinating and comforting but had never seen them or heard them. But over these years in her own home, single and having time to contemplate all of these energies, impacts and disconnects she also had time to notice other things that came in with these ideas.

Chapter 8

Empowerment and Development

Each time she spent time in contemplation over ideas or just asking questions of the universe she got a sense of something responding. Not a voice or even a clear thought but just a very slight feeling. When she was first aware of this change in atmosphere it was very slight. Over these years it had grown and changed into more sensations. Still slight and easily missed but they increased each time she acknowledged them. Sometimes it felt as if someone had entered the room, not scary or intrusive, simply as though there was something else there. A little bit like family or friends, it felt familiar and kind. Nothing was being asked of her just that feeling of support and kindness was surrounding her. As this happened more often with clients and in her own space, she recognised this as a feeling of an ancestor offering information or support. Most of the times it was a feeling in her body or an idea that popped in her head. She did not see or hear them just knew they were there or observed what they were sharing more in sensations and ideas.

The other sensation that grew was much more precise and almost inside of her. Like a channel of light down the centre of her, in the beginning it was a very light sensation. Like truth and reality at the same time. It could come in behind her eyes or within her spine as though the channel of light moved into her body or perhaps opened up. Over time this also became clearer. This feeling of her guides standing behind her while they held space for her to experience and grow grew stronger each time too.

When practicing checking her energy with people over those years she also had become aware of what certainty felt like in her body. Part of this was the feeling of this certainty in her soul and the light that would shine from her centre.

As a working clairvoyant she had been doing this for a few years by trusting herself and her connection so it was a welcome surprise to have a reading with a colleague and have them talk about grounding, cleansing, protection, chakras and all sorts of things that this colleague thought were spiritual basics yet the girl had never come across.

The girl listened to this woman and took all that resonated at the time; the rest would come through when it was needed. She began to consciously clear her aura of energy after being around other people and ask for protection when she was working and even when she was scared. She found healers who could align chakras and clear energy too, and realised that anyone working with energy needs energetic support, so began to include this as part of her regular self-care. Once she felt very unwell after a healing and realised that these too need to be checked against her body like food and the people she chose to be around. They did not need to be regular or a particular modality they just needed to feel right. If she did not feel strong emotionally or physically in daily life she also learned to look for a healing to realign herself.

But the grounding she could not get her head around. Lots of people talked about it around her. She even had a few people give her ideas but she found it easier to almost reach her energy up than down and if felt good and so she did not pay it much attention. A healer she had come to trust told her that if she could ground she could take in more knowledge and gifts and while she was not sure how that would work, she thought it might be worth looking into again.

She was travelling when she laid her hand on a very old wall. With the strangest feeling, like a deep dropping far beneath the ground, she felt like she could feel where this stone had come from. The depth did not feel dark or scary as she would have expected, it was simply old and very deep. The feeling that the centre of her was falling far into the earth felt safe and secure but far more powerful than the light feeling of reaching the energy up.

When she came home from that trip, she played with the feeling of dropping her energy away and as she grounded not only did she feel like she received more energy and information but also she felt stronger and calmer and able to receive more of the love and support her guides and ancestors always offered around her. It would be another year or two until she began to incorporate meditation and grounding regularly into her routine and even then not until she was once again overwhelmed by energy, but eventually she realised that the grounding and the contemplation time were where she received the most support for her body, heart and mind, so learned to give it more value.

Chapter 9

Guides as a support team

Before she got to that space she was still learning to interpret these feelings and impressions that she got when thinking about guides and ancestors. She was still too nervous to want to interact with ancestors but started to try and work with her guides. She asked a lot of people about this. She was offered guide drawings from different people and readings, but nothing really resonated with her.

Eventually the girl met a medium who could see guides. When she started speaking of the image they presented and the things they would say or how they would feel when the girl did certain and specific things, the girl could almost see her guide in her mind`s eye. As if talking to them through another person finally allowed her the confirmation of the thoughts and feelings, and having a description of the guide finally resonate was like meeting an old friend. Now when she wanted to interact with her guide she could bring up an image in her mind or imagine who she was talking to and it seemed easy to recognise the sensation of her centre extending light, resonating or expanding with each connection.

When she was brave enough she realised she needed to reinvestigate her mediumship. She asked for protection and when allowing time to contemplate how that would feel she decided that if they came through her guide at least she would know they were safe and relevant to her journey and not out of her control.

One evening, again when she was on the edge of sleep, the girl was once gain woken by the feeling of someone in the room. First feeling fear then reaching for her guide she asked "Is this agreed with you?". The energy around her became calm and soft and she realised it was by agreement so it must be someone safe. She reached her energy forward and waited. She could almost imagine eyes becoming visible and again fought back the fear. Once she regrouped she reached again and felt the energy around the eyes. Suddenly she recognised them as her grandmother`s eyes and the face became clear, the energy softened and then the experience dissipated. She had never met this grandmother so it was an unusual sensation to know this but it was in her as a certainty. Feeling lighter in her heart she went back to sleep.

When she was very young and frightened, and her mediumship was fresh and unfiltered they would appear to her in a similar vibration as she was in. The difficulty was that the girl was in a traumatic energy in her youth and so they presented in similar ways. Those old experiences had gotten frightening until she asked her guides to shut it down after her sister`s visitations. So, it was with great care that her guides bought it back in this time.

She would be on a date and her partner would talk about his father or uncles and one would pop in smiling and loving and often with naughty story or jolly memory to support what her partner was saying. She would be going to visit a friend and someone would almost give her a nudge to grab something else on the way out and when she got to the next house she would find out why it was needed.

More experiences of mediumship followed of respectful kindness, sharing stories without any emoting or pressure and being in a warm and loving energy that the girl began to enjoy these experiences and the fear was loosened. Sometimes when cooking an old lady would pop in with advice on herbs or of creative solutions to remedy the girls lack of cooking knowledge. Other times when she was talking to friends in pain another old lady would pop in and drop the images into her mind of how to release muscle strains or how to pull stuck energy from a body. They became a helpful part of her day and a welcome if unusual part of her daily life.

As her boundaries here were being strengthened and extended, in turn she was able to step back and ask for space. A dear friend of her partner who had passed simply sat outside with her plants. She never came in as a sign that the girl had a say and supported this energy by showing her how this could be done. This eased the girl`s worries and made it easier to engage in as she really did feel that she was protected, and her guides were protecting her as she learnt.

Another way they brought in learning was in experiencing and giving healings. As an empath she had spent her life receiving information from other people to her detriment. Now she was able to witness their body`s discomfort or minds pain and offer alternative energies, sensations or healing in the same space she could see the damage. They would show it to her in formats that suited each occasion. Like watching movie or TV show can be a gentle way for guides and ancestors to bring in messages, lyrics to a song or repeated phrases throughout a day popping up can be too. Getting to play with energy in daily life rather than in a school environment means that it can be done more gently.

So, the girl would be talking with friends or clients and have the body knowledge of dis-ease and then feel moved to physically or energetically shift and support them. As people agreed for her to work on them this became clearer and easier to shift each time and over the years several modalities developed. Sometimes they were delivered by the guides of that client so far from her usual style. Other times clients would come to her for her own version of realignments and rejuvenation.

As long as the girl remembered to disconnect and toss away the other persons` energies when she finished, she found this to be energizing and beautiful. It was no longer making her sick alongside them and she was able to very deeply feel what was out of balance or injured and offer whatever healing their guides permitted. Sometimes the lesson was not to be able to heal or adjust anything, that until they moved through the lesson they were in themselves that her interference would not work. Other times it was because her clients had worked on releasing the emotional pattern that was holding pain in place or manifesting illness and the girl was simply their own guides` release option at the end of their lesson.

Always it was a loving and beautiful experience and the girl was now happy and often filled with joy. It was a strange place to be at the far end of the experience from where she had started.

Now with respect and appreciation for why she needed to learn through so many deep experiences, so was able to trust herself and others to be in the right space and place on their journeys, without control or interference. She could see the love and learning in all these situations and when she went through difficult times in life, she was usually able to regroup and see the blessing in the journey, learn faster, allow emotions to come up and be experienced, investigated or released.

To be able to disengage from the energy that other people threw her way and know it was not about her gave her freedom and calmness in her life. She was able to live in a very sensitive and open way that resonated with her without feeling exposed or insecure.

My wish for you

The feeling of joy when you learn to you trust your instincts is a signal you are on the right path. If it brings you joy or makes your soul light up then it is worth your attention. Every time you stop and check something with you your self-confidence and communication with yourself and guides or ancestors can increase.

Take the time to listen to you. You do not have to make anything fit your mind or change the way you think and feel to fit someone else`s. Just see what is going on in your head, heart and body and then chose to love yourself. The choices of what to do next come easier and better each time.

About the Author

She grew up in a big family with many ups and downs and has had life events all designed to add to her learning. These have been used to gain a fuller view of experiences and observe the energy around them to learn what we can do to create positive growth. A healer who has always had these psychic gifts.

Channelling clairvoyance in many forms including mediumship, empathy and all with deep healing she has been working with people for decades to offer support and share information, but her main focus is openly talking about experience and knowledge with others to make our journeys easier and more transparent.

Sharing understanding with people of their gifts and supporting them in accessing and extending them with integrity builds confidence and self-esteem in place of anxiety and stress.

www.calicodawn.com

https://www.facebook.com/calicodawnauthor